HAL•LEONARD®

GUITAR
PLAY-ALONG

AUDIO ACCESS INCLUDED

PLAYBACK+
Speed • Pitch • Balance • Loop

VOL. 173

Trans-Siberian Orchestra

FEATURES AUTHENTIC RECORDINGS!

To access audio visit:
www.halleonard.com/mylibrary

Enter Code
1088-4238-6022-5066

HAL•LEONARD®
7777 W. BLUEMOUND RD. P.O. BOX 13819 MILWAUKEE, WI 53213

ISBN: 978-1-4803-4552-2

In Australia Contact:
Hal Leonard Australia Pty. Ltd.
4 Lentara Court
Cheltenham, Victoria, 3192 Australia
Email: ausadmin@halleonard.com.au

T0050651

Visit Hal Leonard Online at
www.halleonard.com

Guitar Notation Legend

THE MUSICAL STAFF shows pitches and rhythms and is divided by bar lines into measures. Pitches are named after the first seven letters of the alphabet.

TABLATURE graphically represents the guitar fingerboard. Each horizontal line represents a string, and each number represents a fret.

4th string, 2nd fret   1st & 2nd strings open, played together   open D chord

---

HALF-STEP BEND: Strike the note and bend up 1/2 step.

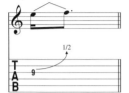

WHOLE-STEP BEND: Strike the note and bend up one step.

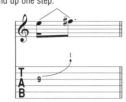

GRACE NOTE BEND: Strike the note and immediately bend up as indicated.

SLIGHT (MICROTONE) BEND: Strike the note and bend up 1/4 step.

BEND AND RELEASE: Strike the note and bend up as indicated, then release back to the original note. Only the first note is struck.

PRE-BEND: Bend the note as indicated, then strike it.

VIBRATO: The string is vibrated by rapidly bending and releasing the note with the fretting hand.

PALM MUTING: The note is partially muted by the pick hand lightly touching the string(s) just before the bridge.

HAMMER-ON: Strike the first (lower) note with one finger, then sound the higher note (on the same string) with another finger by fretting it without picking.

PULL-OFF: Place both fingers on the notes to be sounded. Strike the first note and without picking, pull the finger off to sound the second (lower) note.

LEGATO SLIDE: Strike the first note and then slide the same fret-hand finger up or down to the second note. The second note is not struck.

SHIFT SLIDE: Same as legato slide, except the second note is struck.

TRILL: Very rapidly alternate between the notes indicated by continuously hammering on and pulling off.

TAPPING: Hammer ("tap") the fret indicated with the pick-hand index or middle finger and pull off to the note fretted by the fret hand.

NATURAL HARMONIC: Strike the note while the fret-hand lightly touches the string directly over the fret indicated.

PINCH HARMONIC: The note is fretted normally and a harmonic is produced by adding the edge of the thumb or the tip of the index finger of the pick hand to the normal pick attack.

TREMOLO PICKING: The note is picked as rapidly and continuously as possible.

VIBRATO BAR DIVE AND RETURN: The pitch of the note or chord is dropped a specified number of steps (in rhythm), then returned to the original pitch.

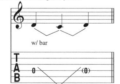

VIBRATO BAR SCOOP: Depress the bar just before striking the note, then quickly release the bar.

VIBRATO BAR DIP: Strike the note and then immediately drop a specified number of steps, then release back to the original pitch.

Additional Musical Definitions

 (accent)
- Accentuate note (play it louder).

 (staccato)
- Play the note short.

D.S. al Coda
- Go back to the sign (‰), then play until the measure marked "*To Coda*," then skip to the section labelled "**Coda**."

D.C. al Fine
- Go back to the beginning of the song and play until the measure marked "*Fine*" (end).

Fill
- Label used to identify a brief melodic figure which is to be inserted into the arrangement.

N.C.
- Harmony is implied.

- Repeat measures between signs.

- When a repeated section has different endings, play the first ending only the first time and the second ending only the second time.

CONTENTS

Christmas Eve/Sarajevo 12/24

Music by Paul O'Neill and Robert Kinkel

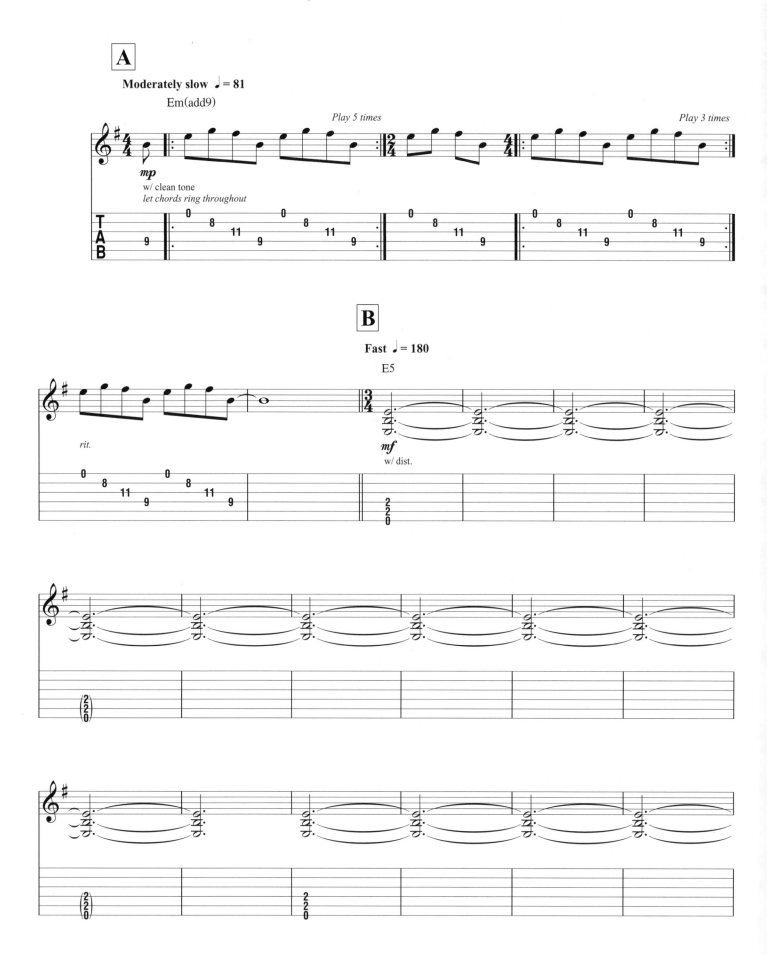

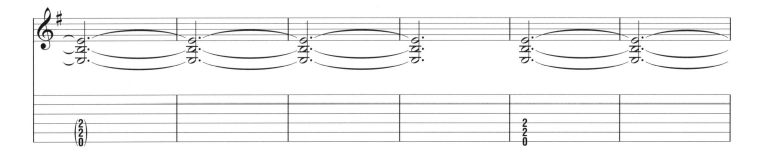

C

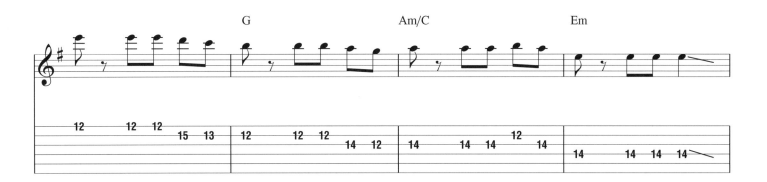

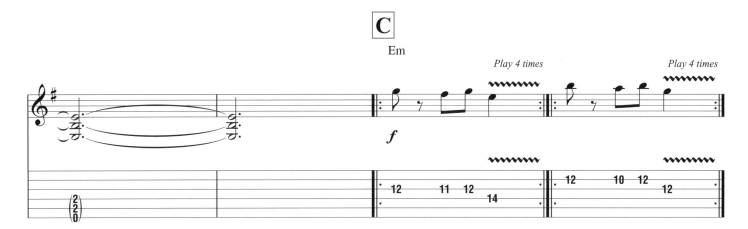

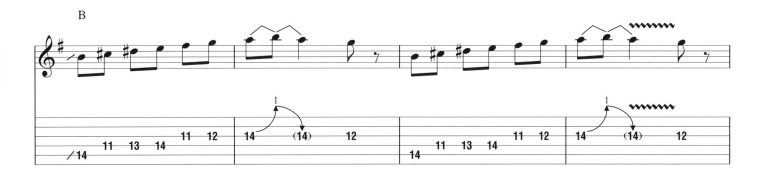

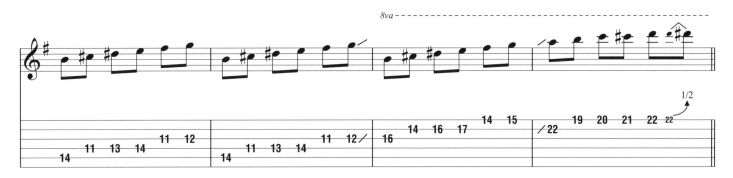

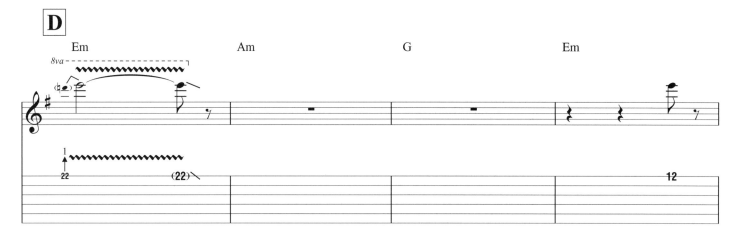

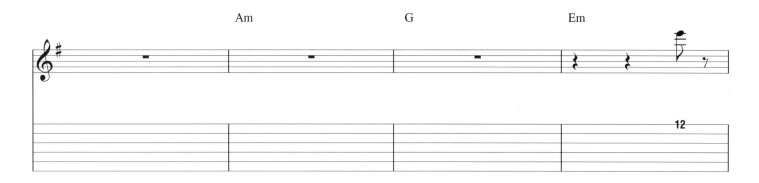

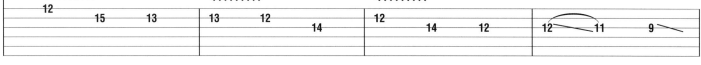

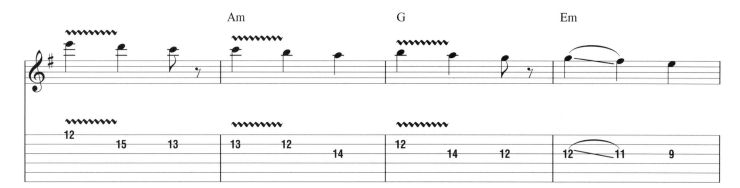

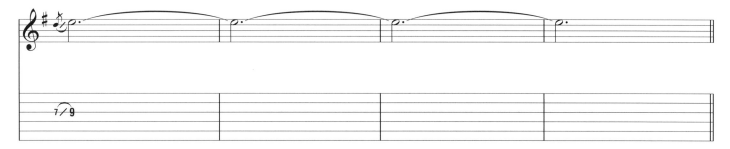

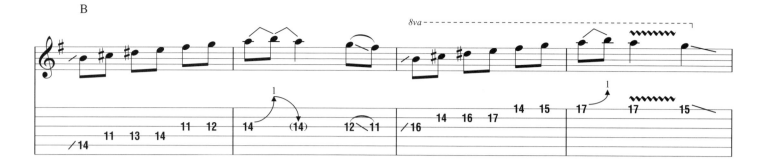

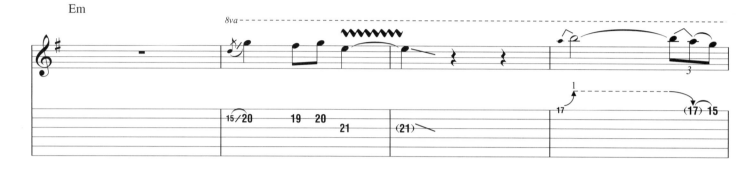

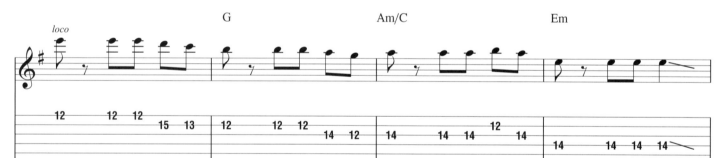

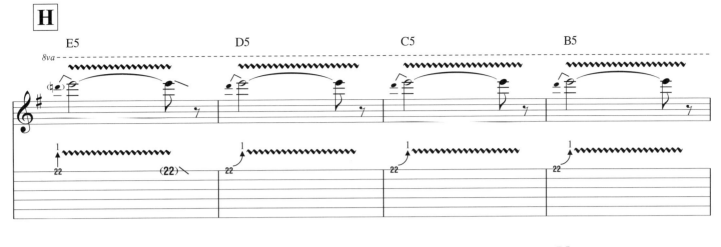

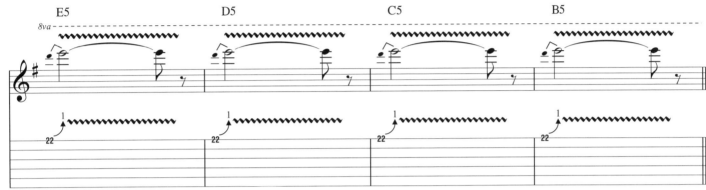

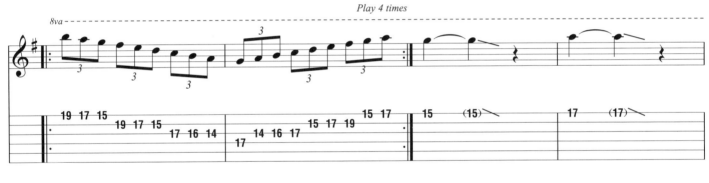

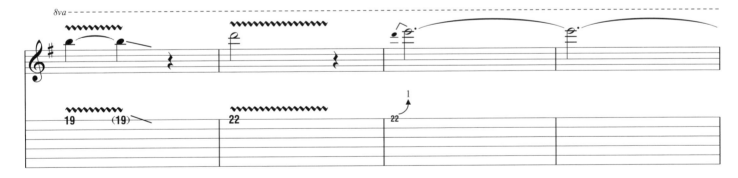

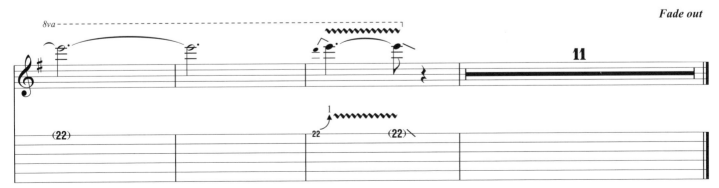

Dreams of Fireflies

Music by Paul O'Neill

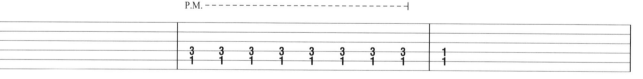

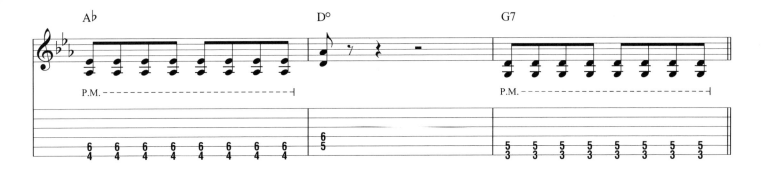

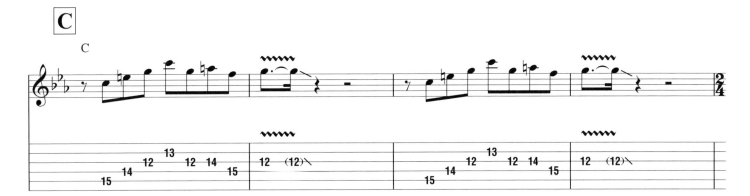

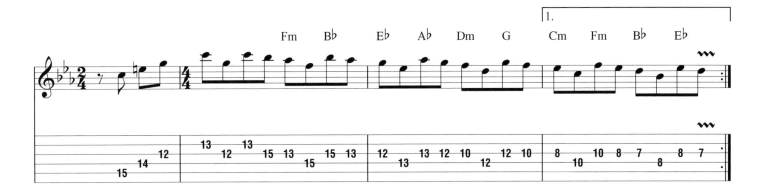

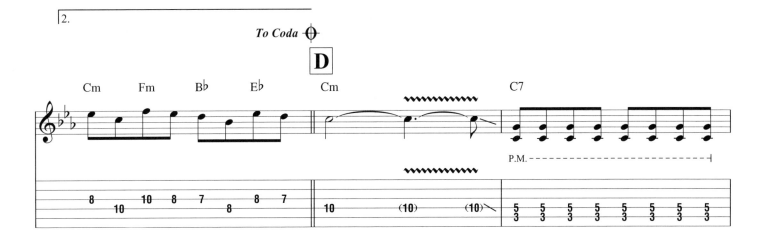

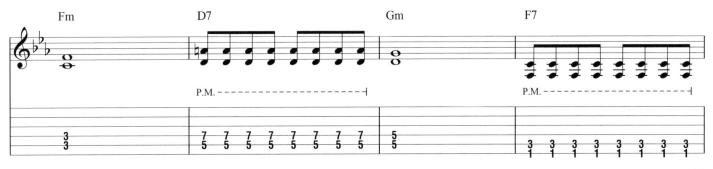

*w/ delay

*Set for quarter-note regeneration w/ moderate feedback.

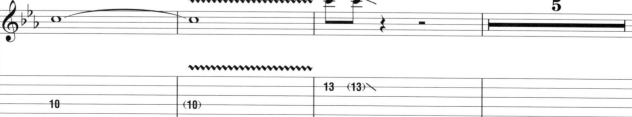

A Mad Russian's Christmas

Music by Paul O'Neill, Robert Kinkel and Peter Ilyich Tchaikovsky

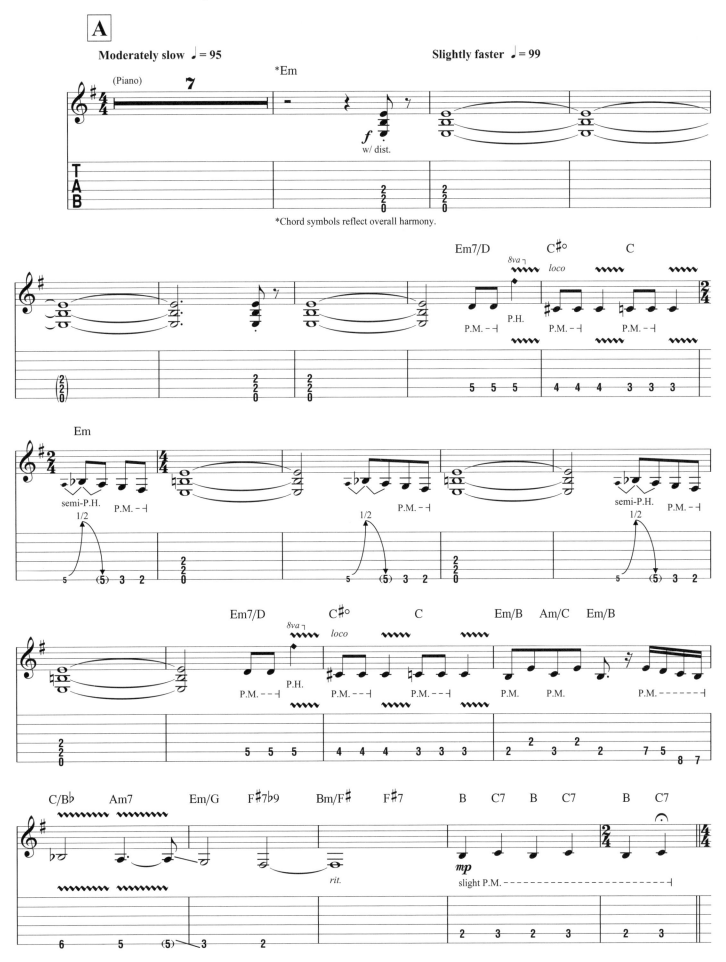

*Chord symbols reflect overall harmony.

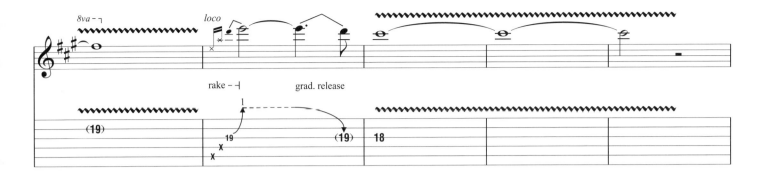

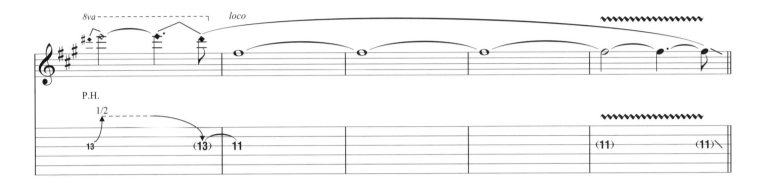

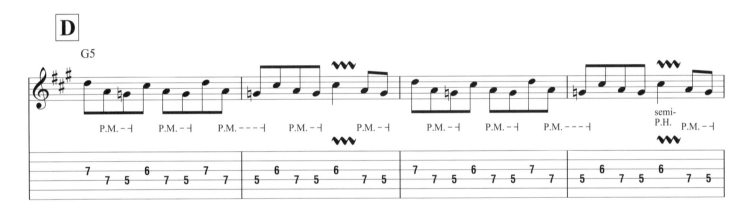

D

E

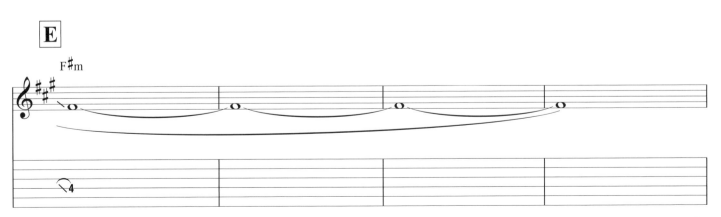

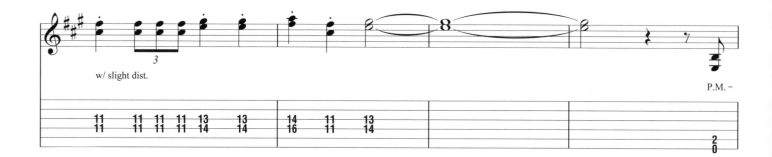

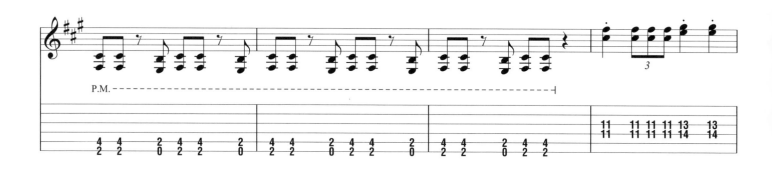

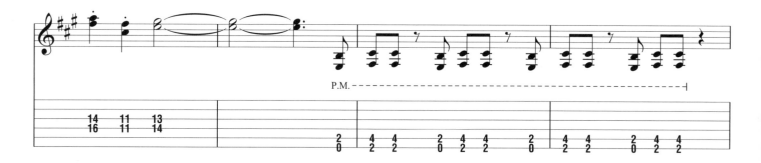

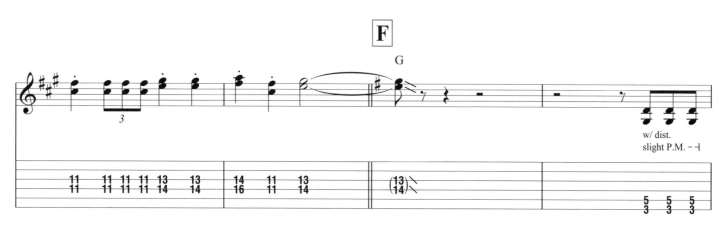

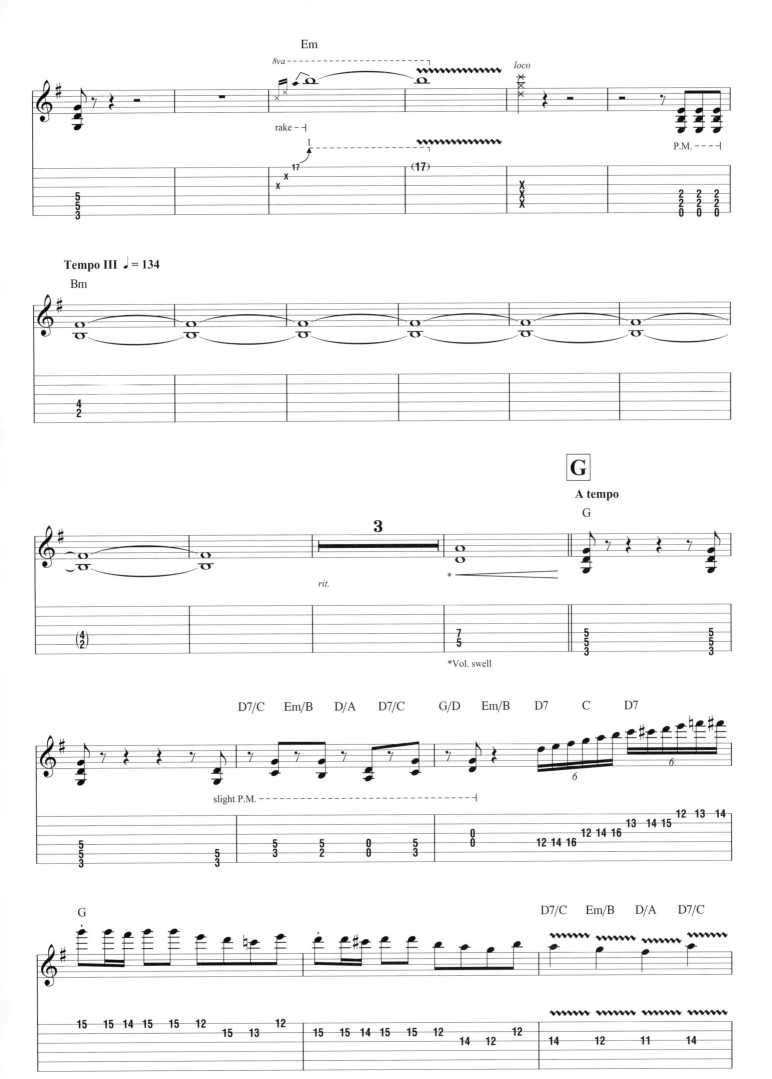

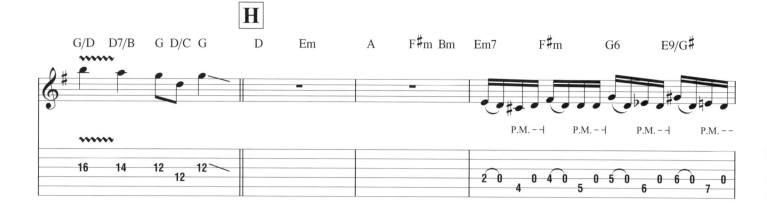

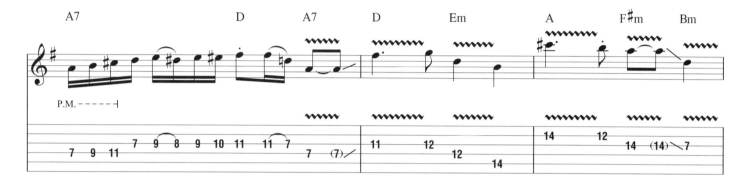

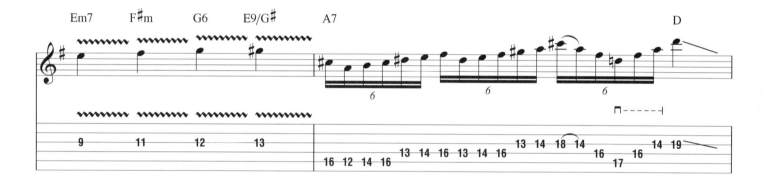

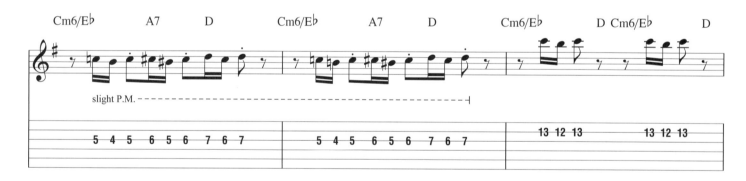

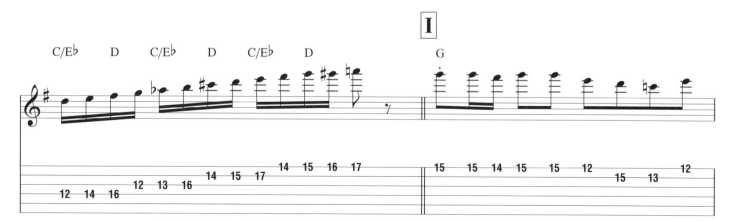

18

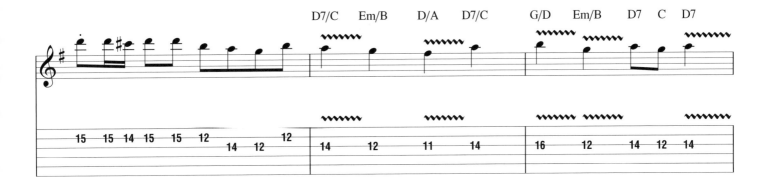

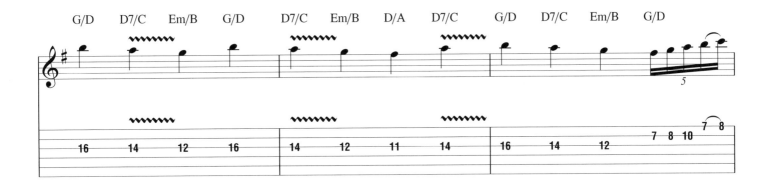

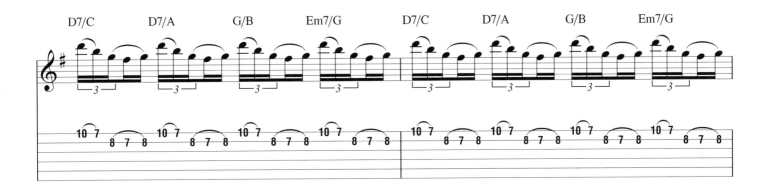

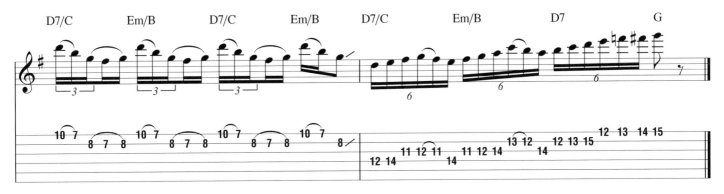

First Snow

Music by Paul O'Neill

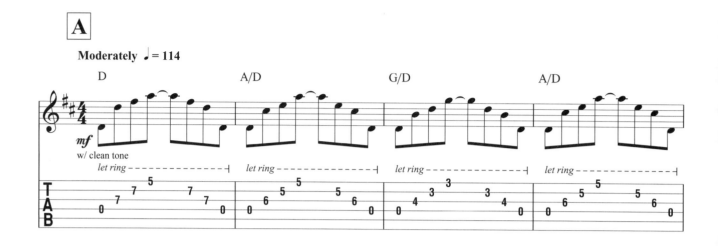

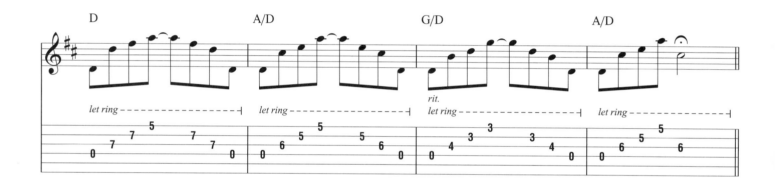

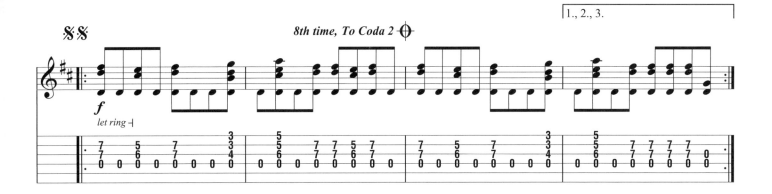

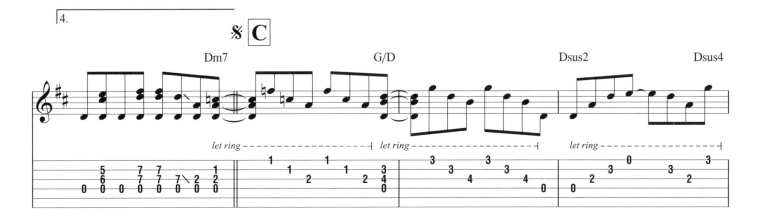

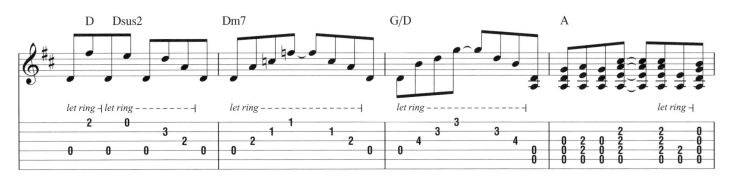

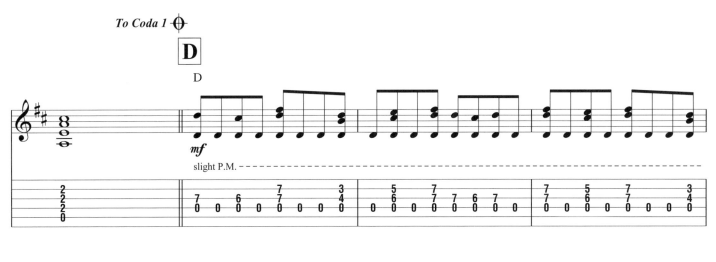

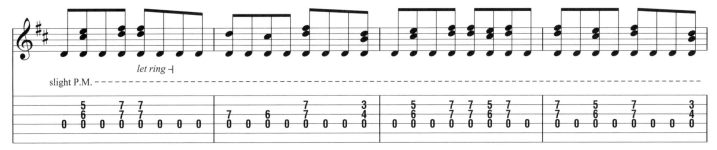

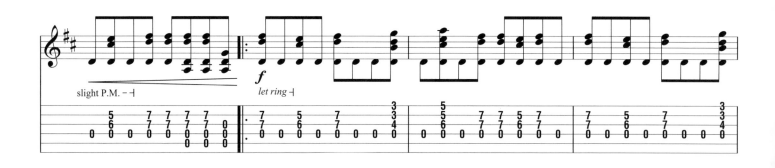

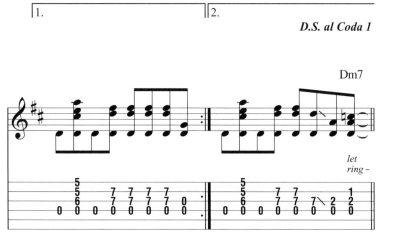

D.S. al Coda 1

Coda 1

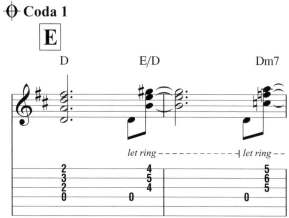

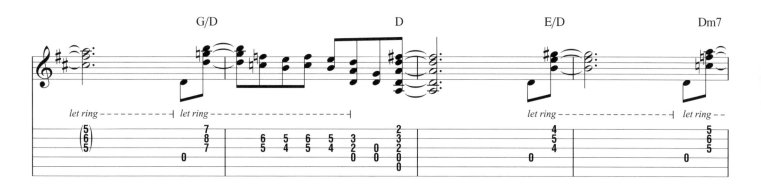

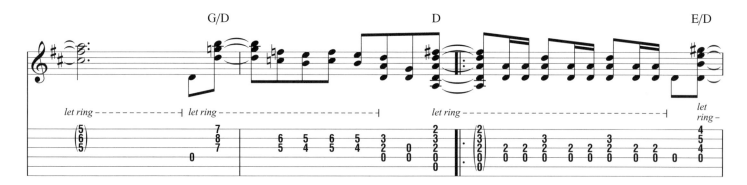

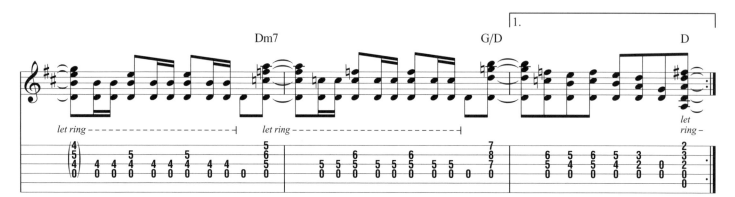

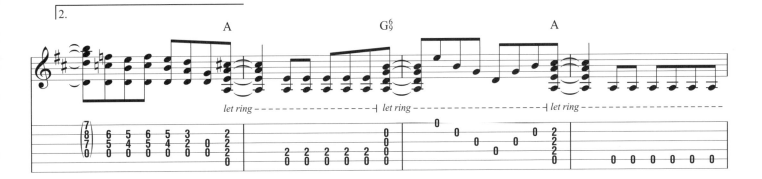

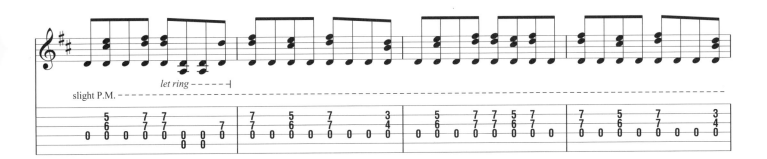

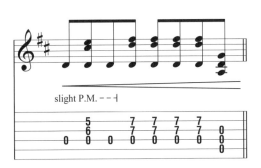

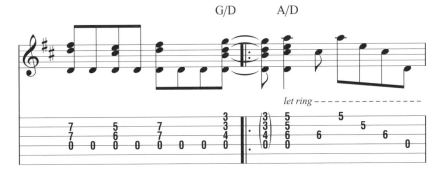

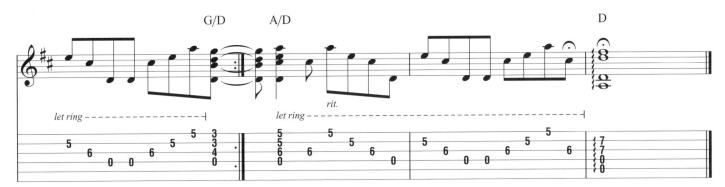

The Mountain

By Edvard Grieg, Paul O'Neill and Jon Oliva

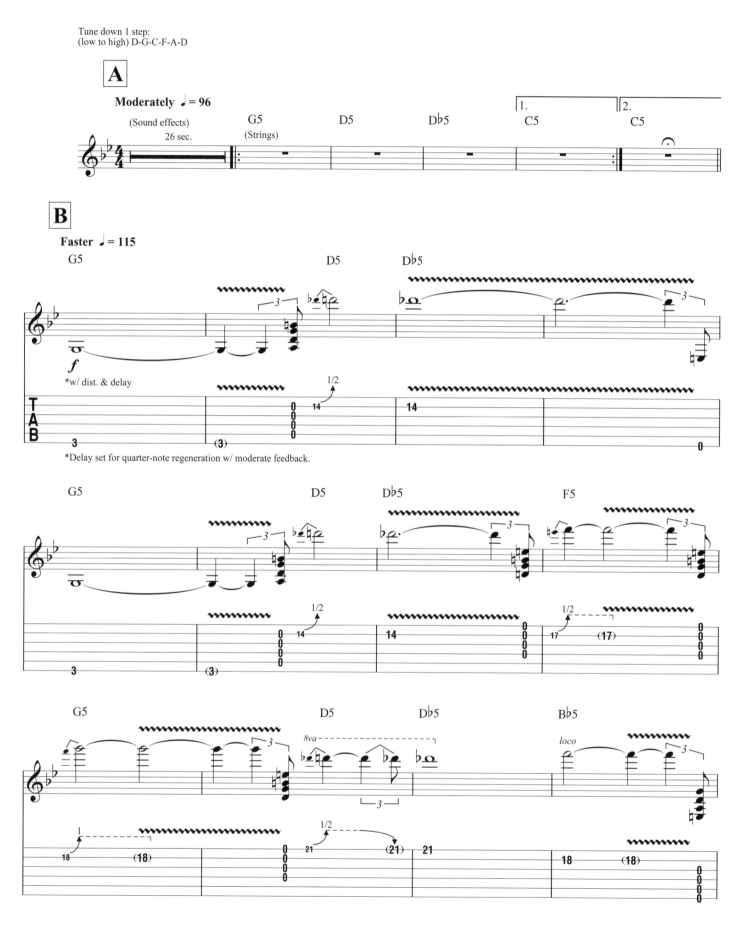

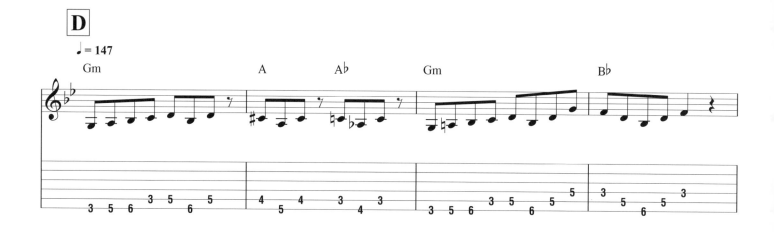

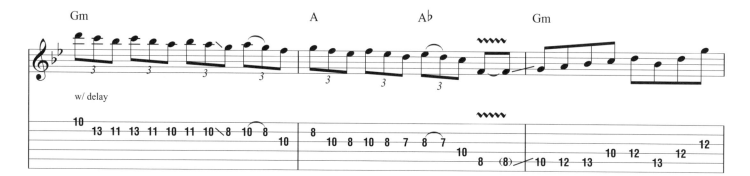

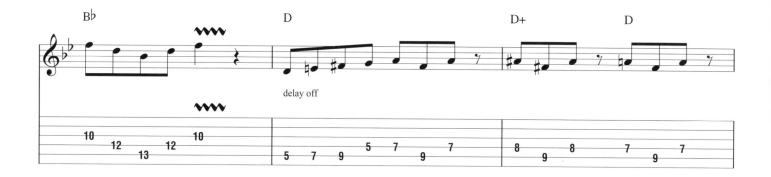

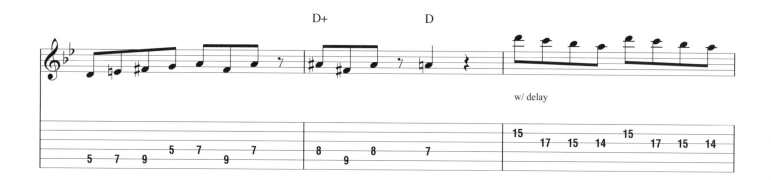

E

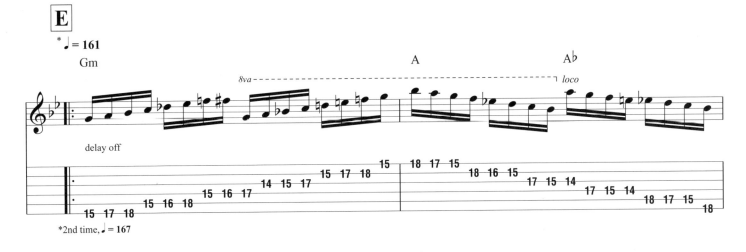

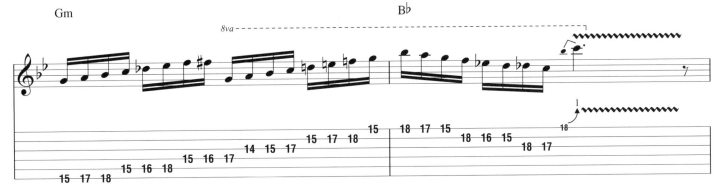

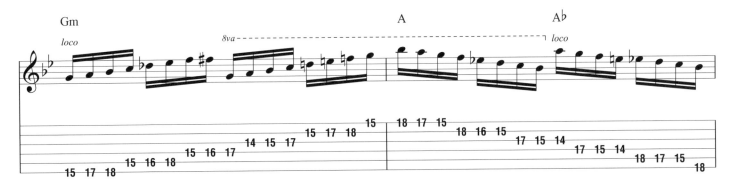

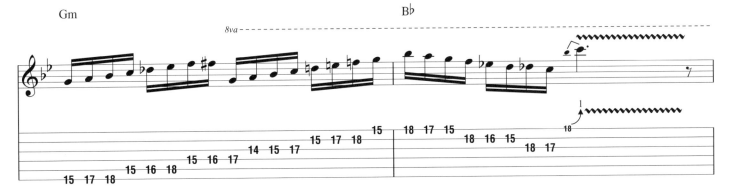

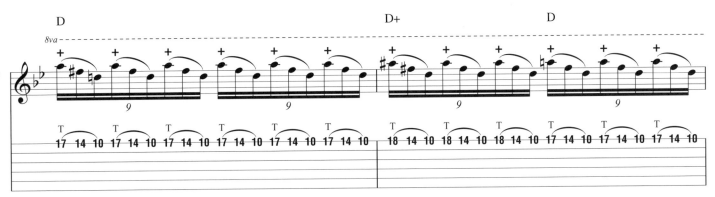

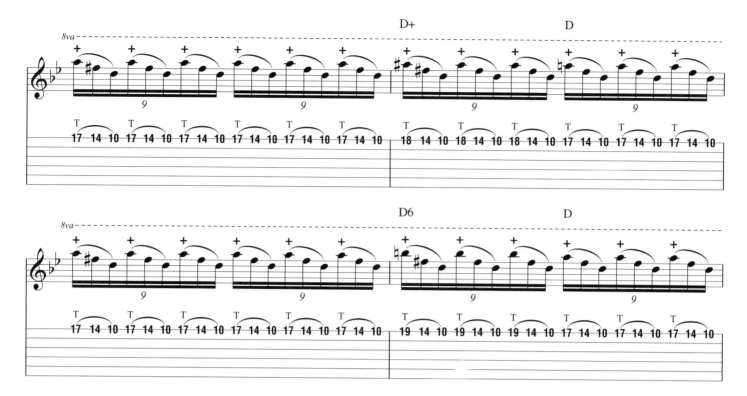

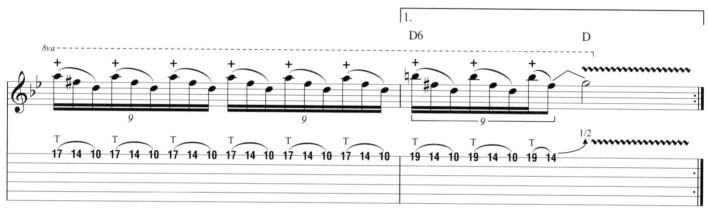

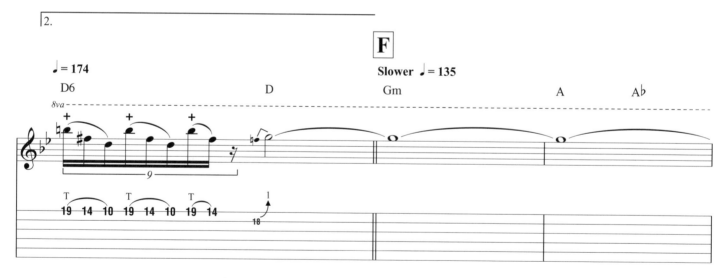

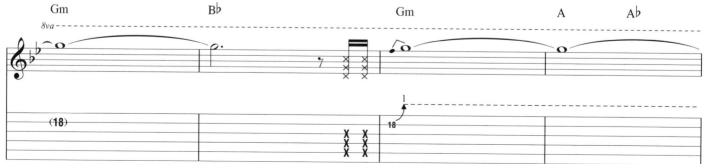

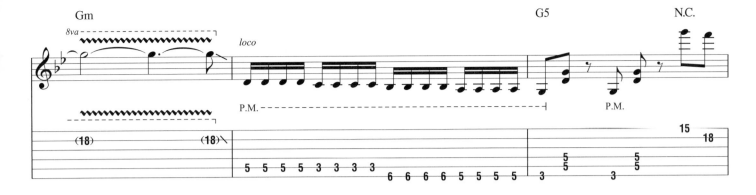

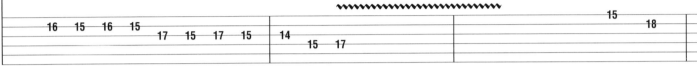

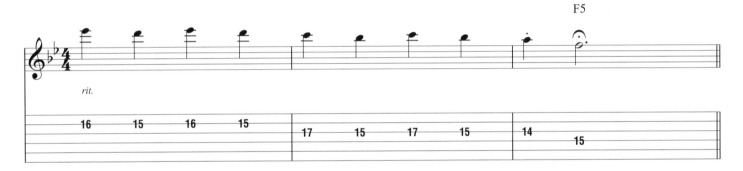

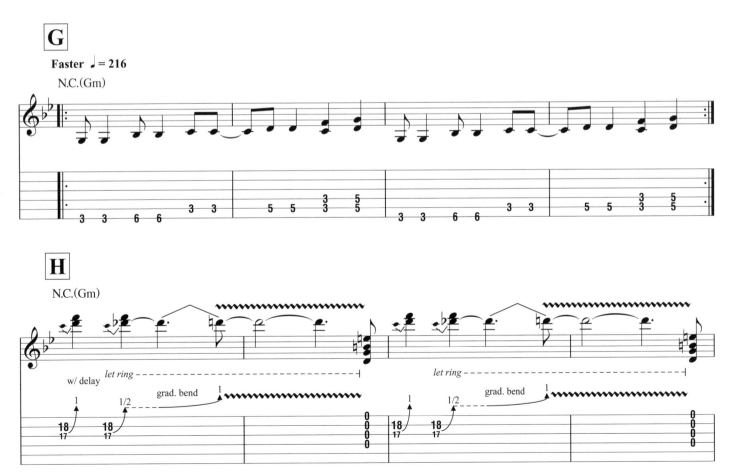

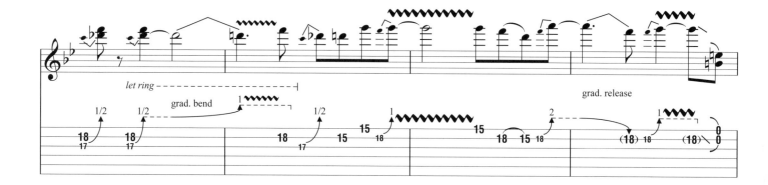

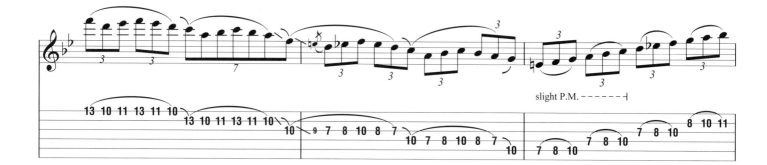

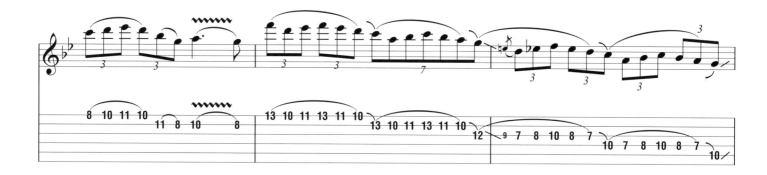

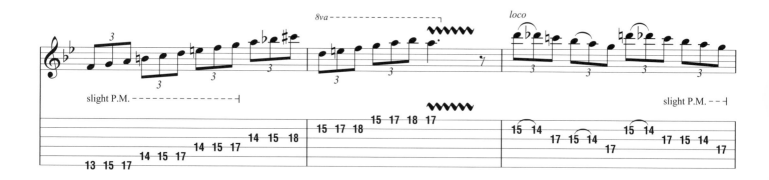

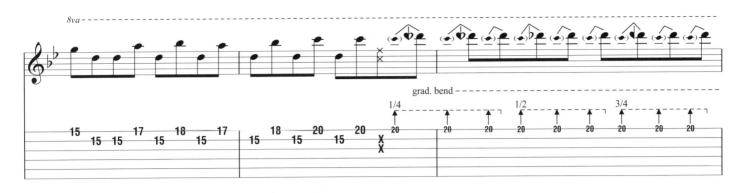

I

N.C.(Dm)

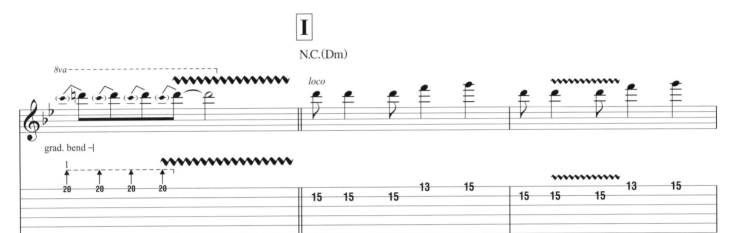

C5

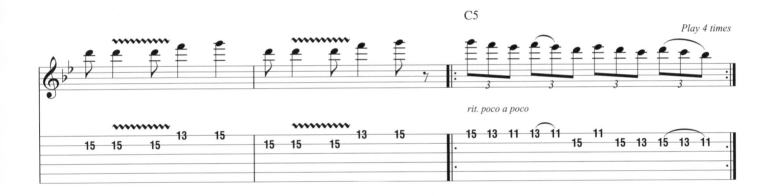

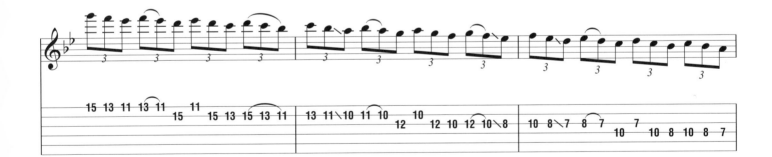

G5

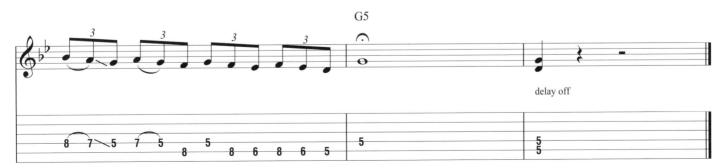

Mozart and Memories

Music by Paul O'Neill and Jon Oliva
(Based upon SYMPHONY NO. 25 by Wolfgang Amadeus Mozart)

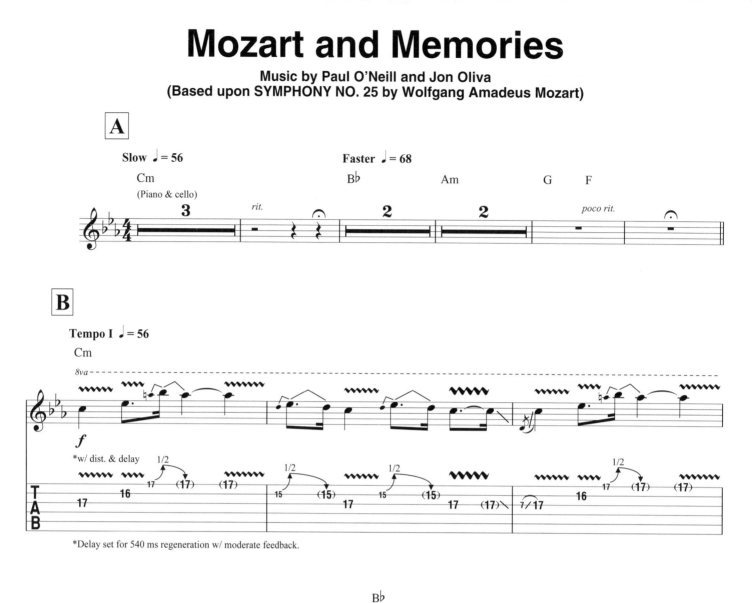

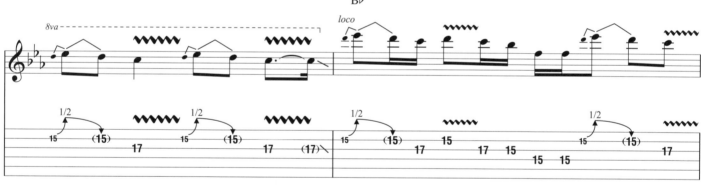

*Delay set for 540 ms regeneration w/ moderate feedback.

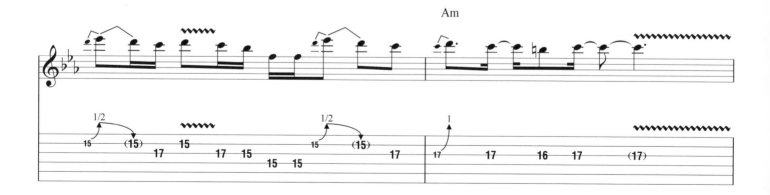

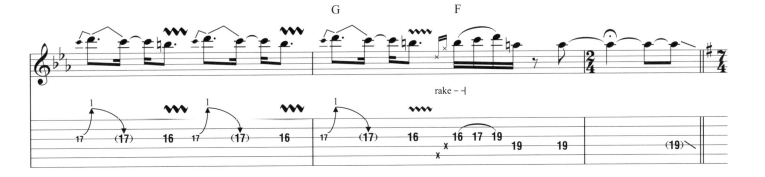

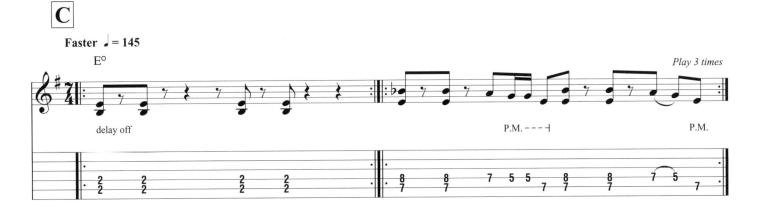

C

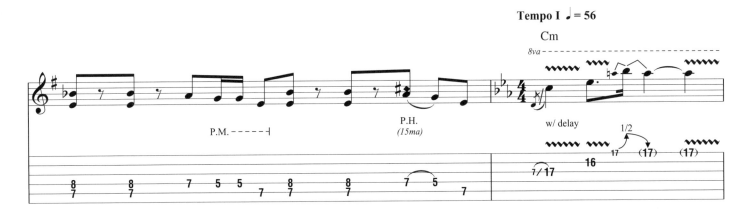

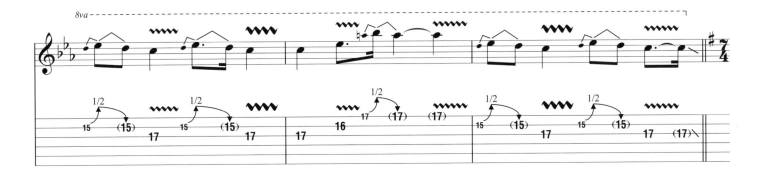

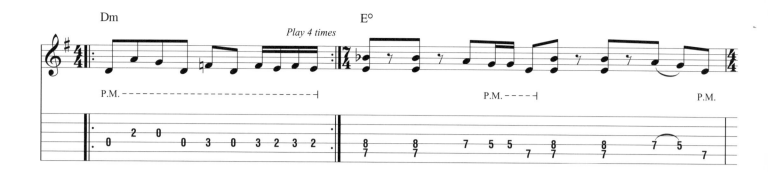

D

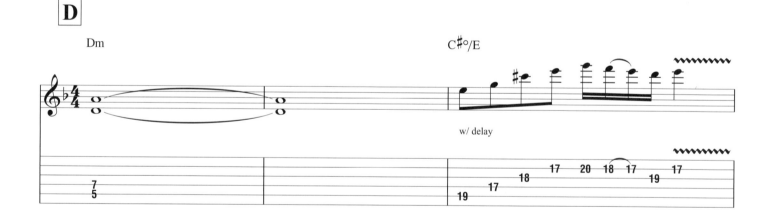

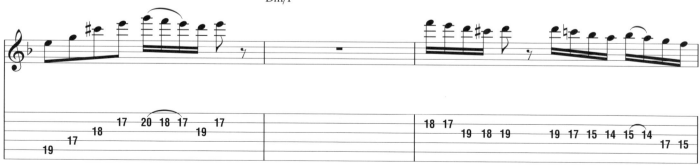

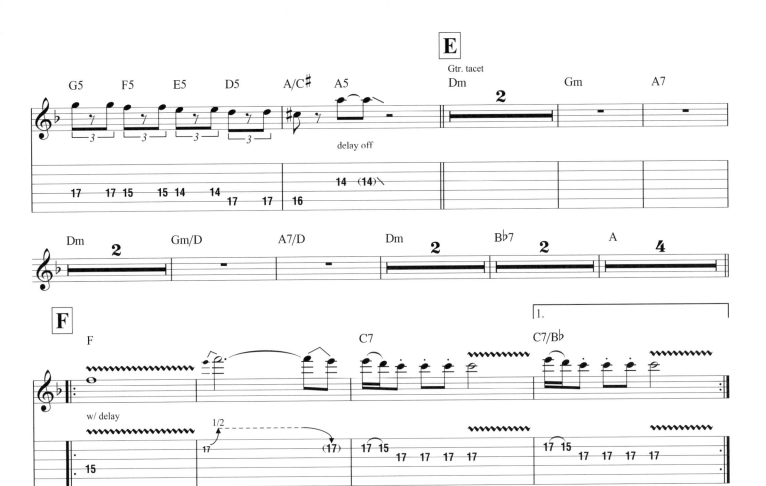

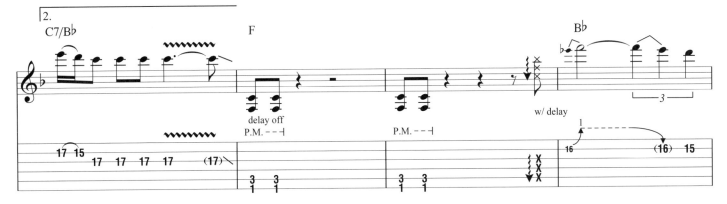

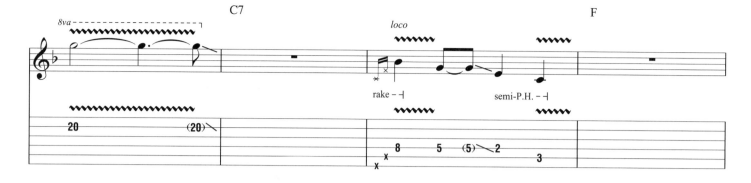

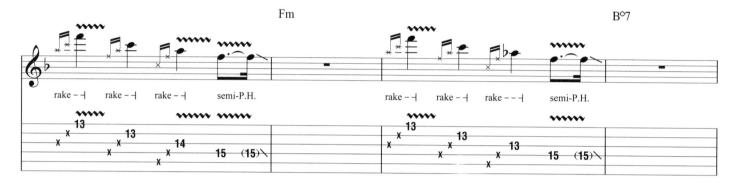

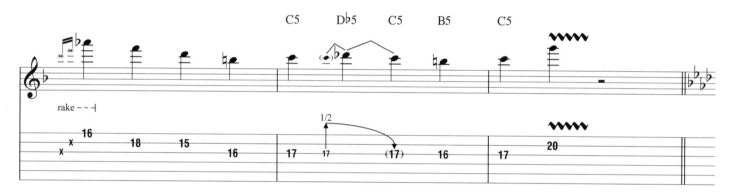

G

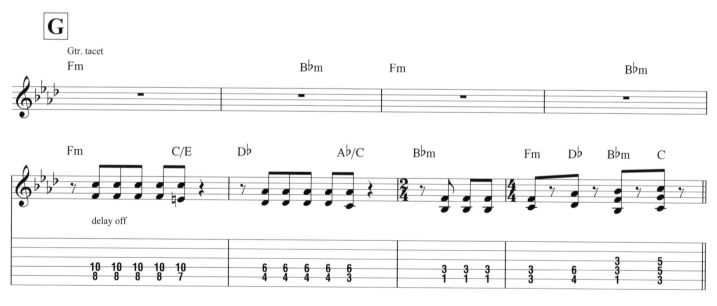

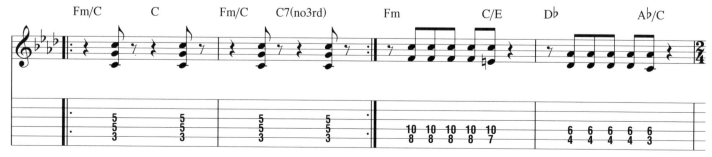

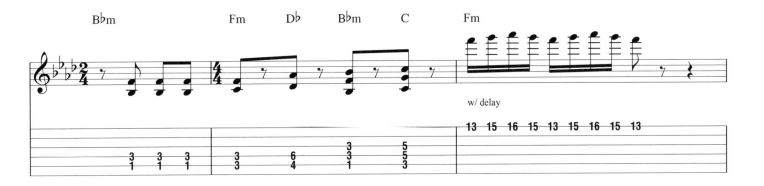

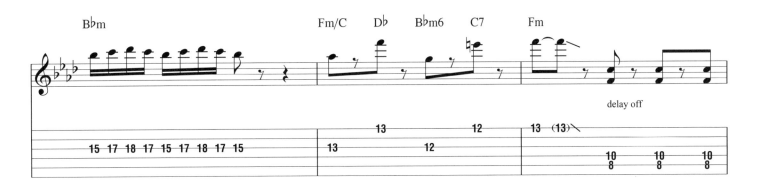

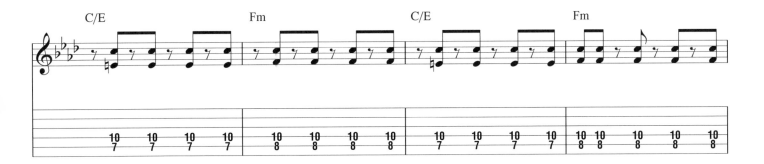

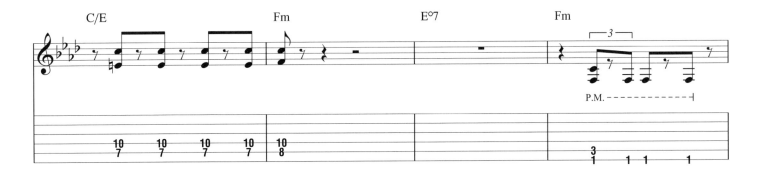

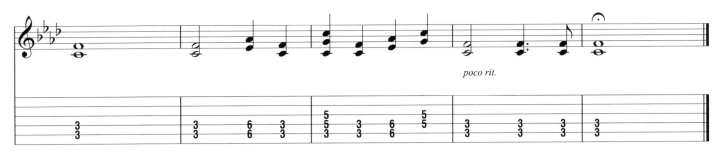

Siberian Sleigh Ride

Music by Paul O'Neill

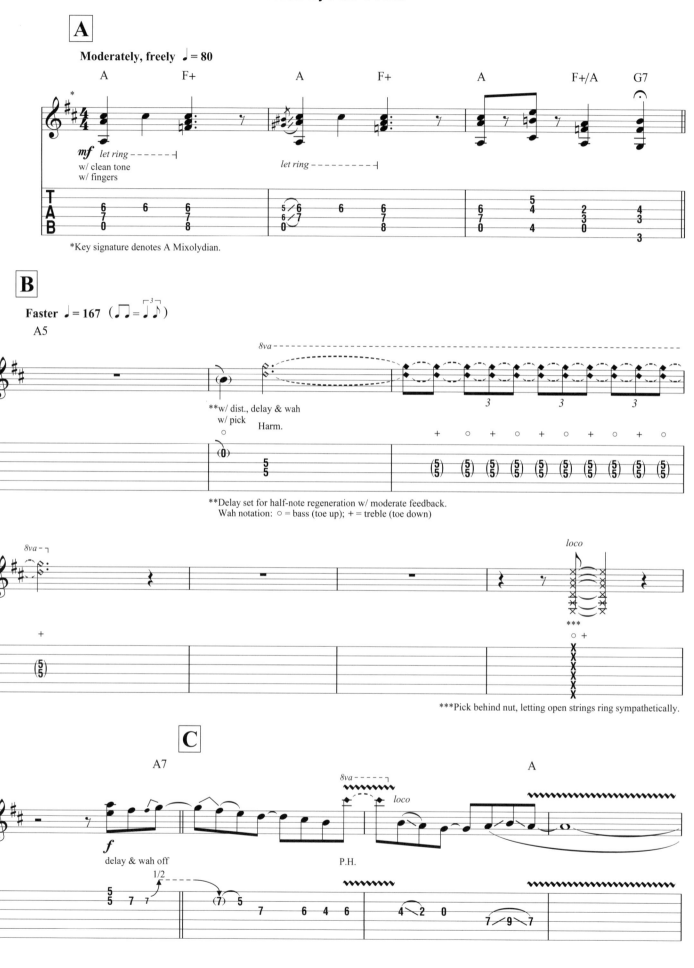

*Key signature denotes A Mixolydian.

**w/ dist., delay & wah

**Delay set for half-note regeneration w/ moderate feedback.
Wah notation: ○ = bass (toe up); + = treble (toe down)

***Pick behind nut, letting open strings ring sympathetically.

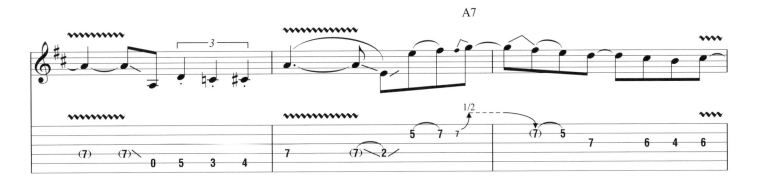

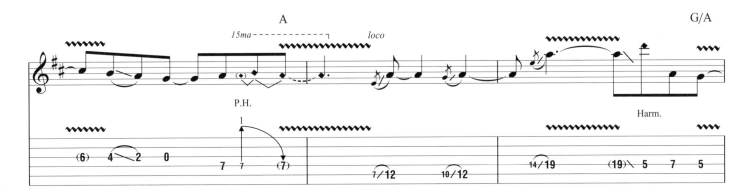

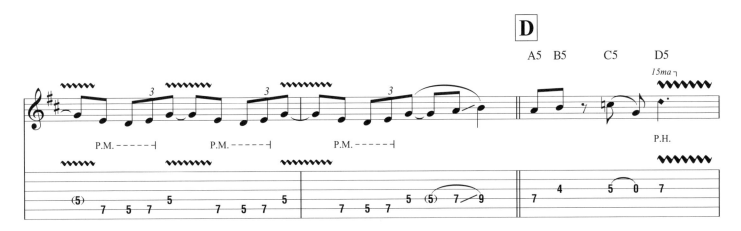

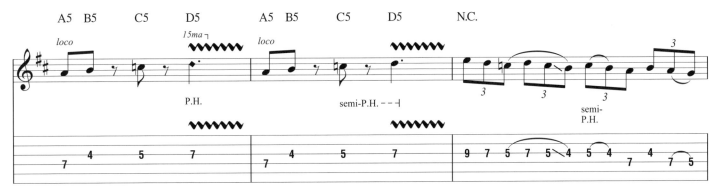

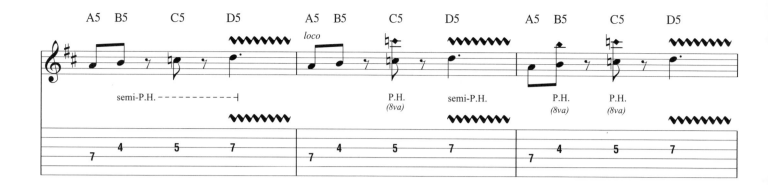

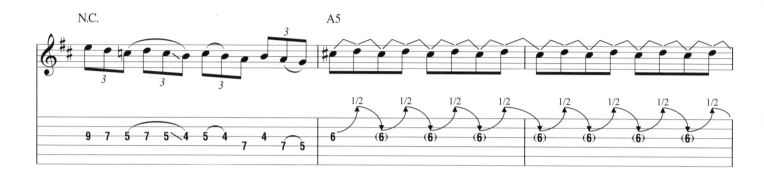

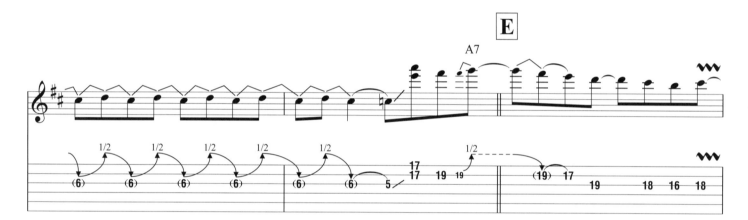

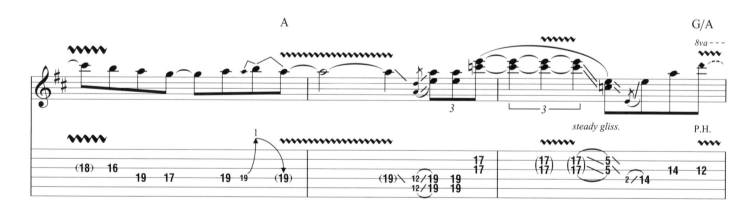

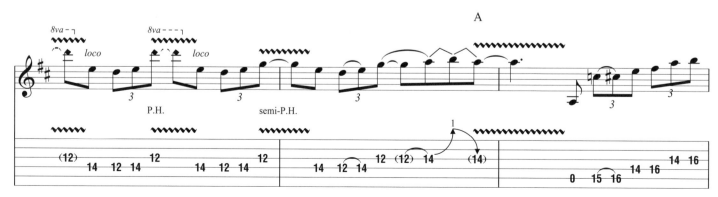

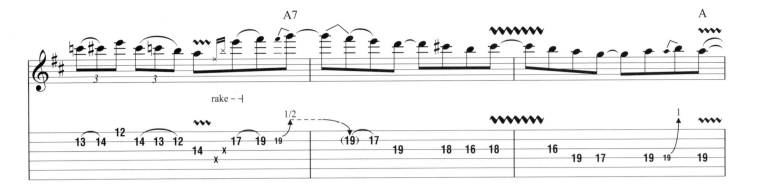

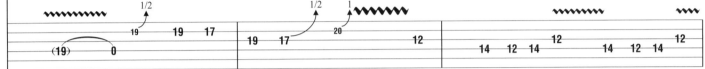

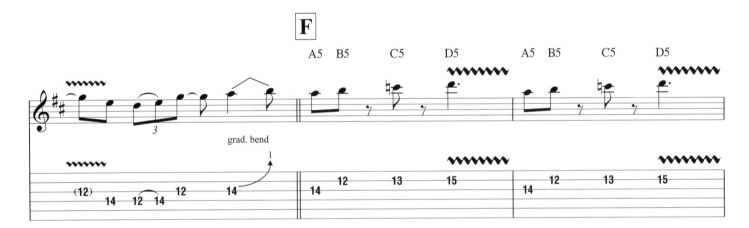

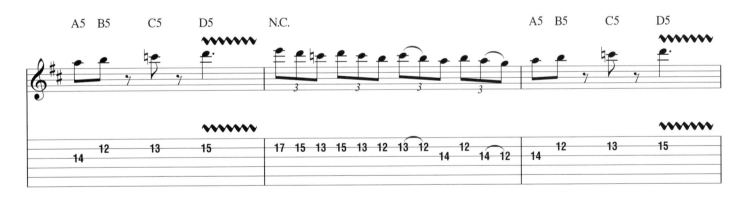

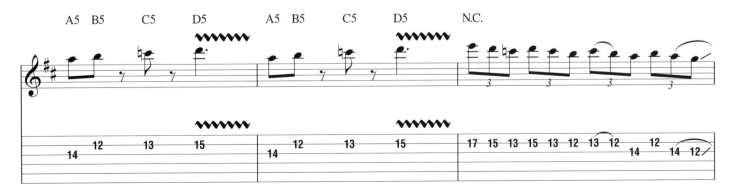

Aadd9

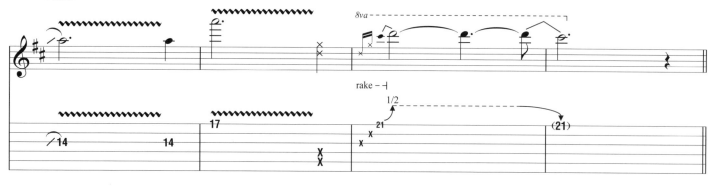

G

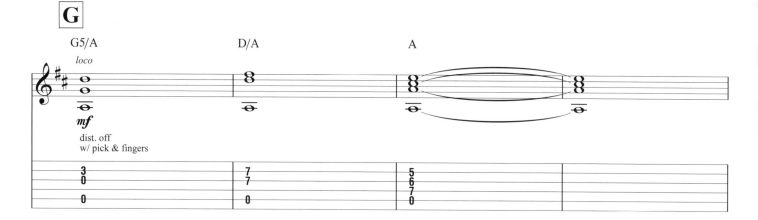

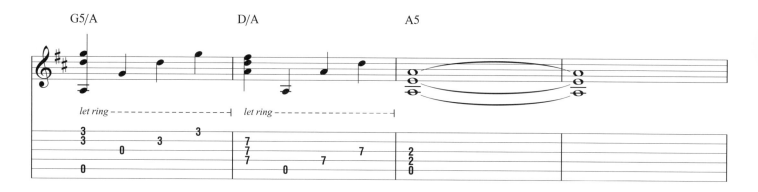

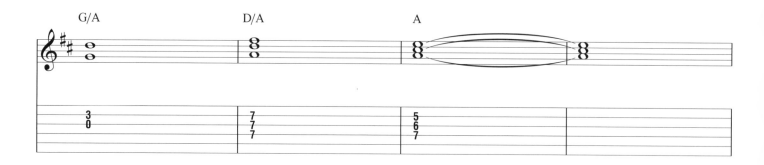

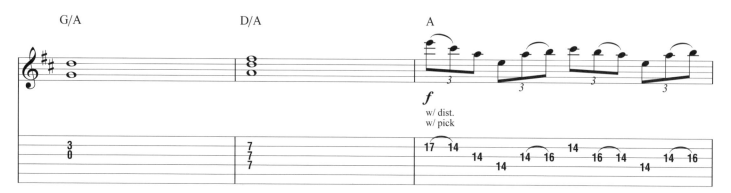

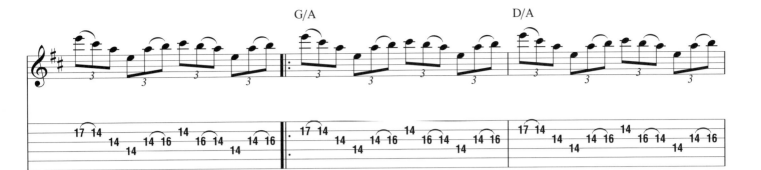

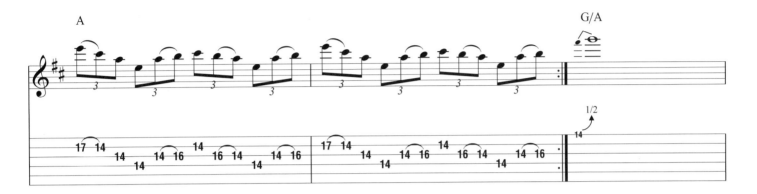

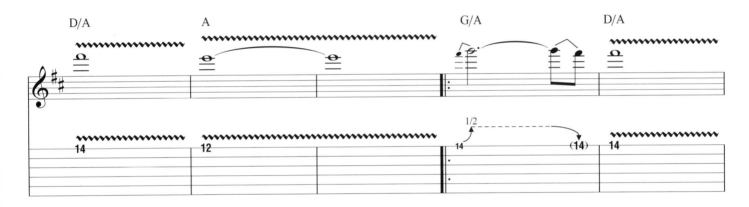

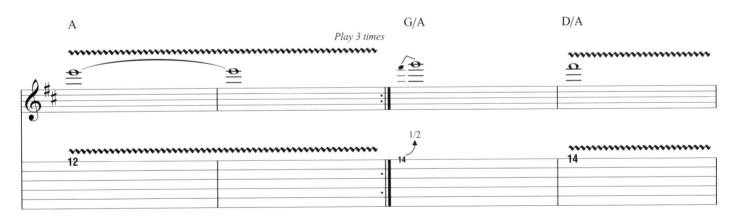

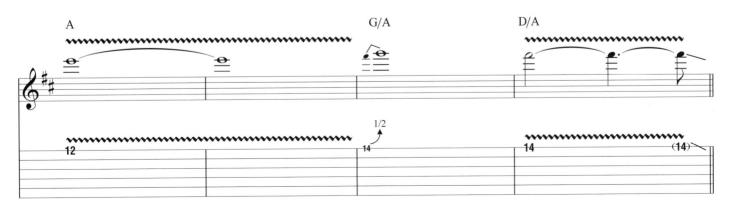

H

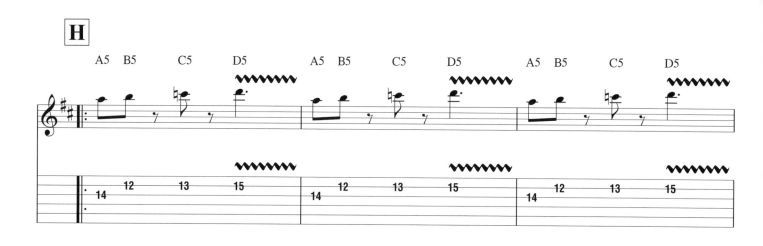

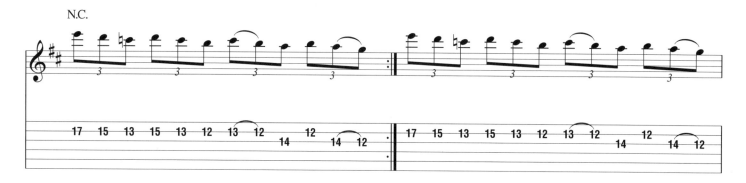

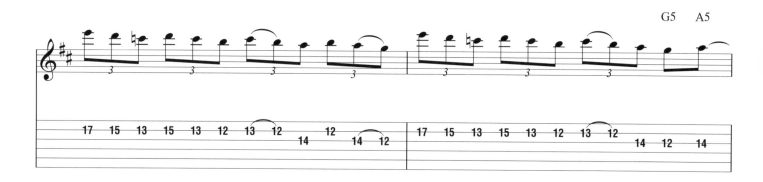

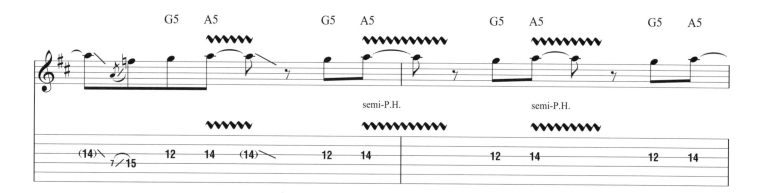

Wizards in Winter

Music by Paul O'Neill and Robert Kinkel

*Chord symbols reflect overall harmony.

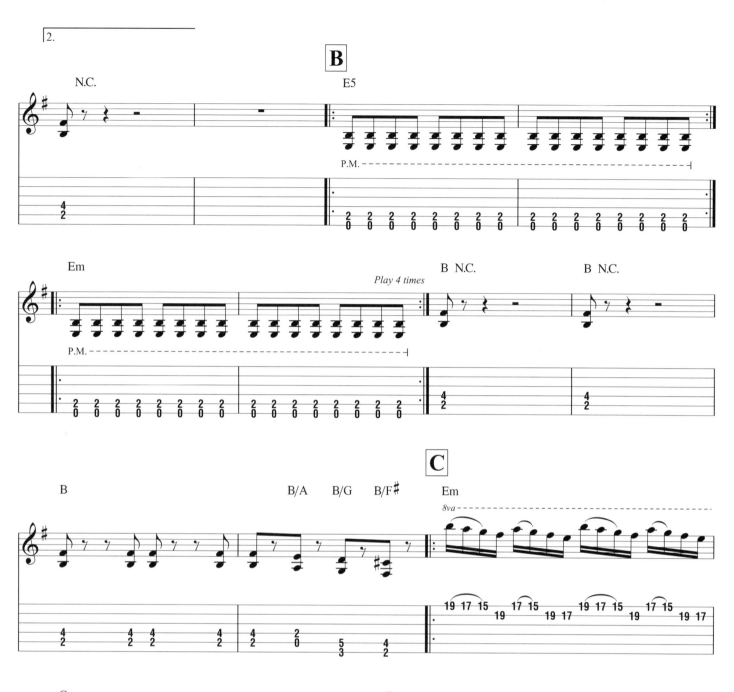

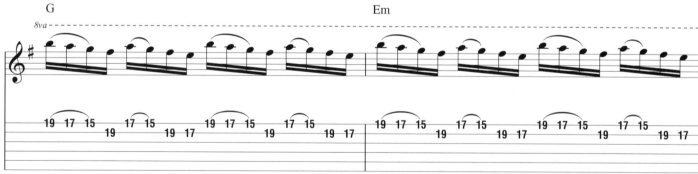

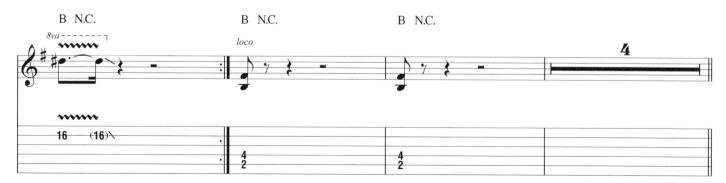

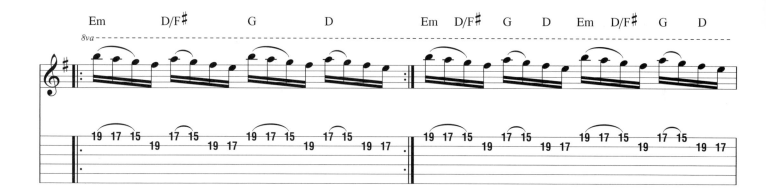

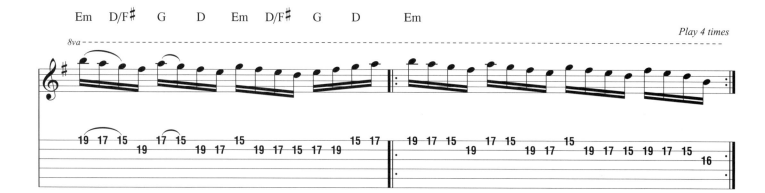

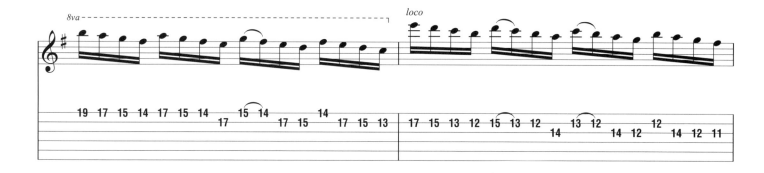

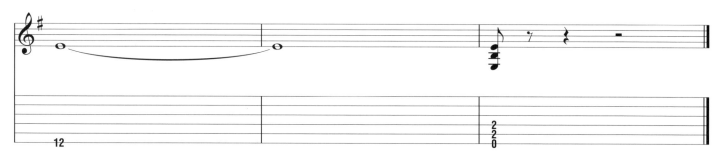